VIKING
EMAIL MARKETING

Chapter 1:

Intro to Email Marketing

What is Email Marketing?

Email marketing, at it's core, is pretty straight forward. It's the use of email messages sent to a list of subscribers to advertise or promote brands, products, offers, events, or pretty much anything you want. Now that "core" definition of email marketing may be simple, but email marketing has come a long way in recent years and there's actually quite a bit more to it than that, today. We'll be discussing those advances later in this guide, but first, let's go over WHY you need email marketing in your business.

Why Email Marketing?

The need for email marketing is one of those things you just can't argue with because the numbers are just too clear and astounding to ignore. According to a report by DMA, the average return on investment (ROI) for email marketing these days is $38 for every $1 spent. And 80% of business professionals report growth in customer acquisition and retention resulting from email marketing. There's nothing else like it. Not even social media comes close. Leads are twice as likely to opt-in to your email list than they are to engage with your business on Facebook. And if you thought social media and search engines were the key to growing your business, think again. Email conversion rates are higher than both search and social combined!

This should come as no surprise, really. Consumers have repeatedly insisted that they LIKE getting promotional messages via email. Over 70% of consumers say email is their preferred channel for business communication and 60% even say they want to receive your marketing emails weekly or MORE often. So, in light of all the recent trends and data, there's really no questioning the critical importance of email marketing in your business. If you're not using email marketing in your business, it's time to start, right now. The only question is where to start.

Where to start Email Marketing.

So, as you've probably guessed, robust email marketing operations can't exactly be run from your personal email account. You need an actual email marketing platform, commonly called an "autoresponder" service. These platforms can handle a wide range of email marketing processes from basic things like initial autoresponder sequences and weekly newsletter scheduling to more advanced stuff like automation workflows (which we'll discuss later).

Popular platforms that can handle most of these functions include:

GetResponse

Aweber

ActiveCampaign

ConstantContact

iContact

CampaignMonitor

MailChimp

SendReach

ConvertKit

SendLane

SendGrid

VerticalResponse

MarketHero

InfusionSoft

Ontraport

As you can see, there are a ton of email marketing platforms out there for you to choose from. You should dedicate a day or two to researching each one, comparing features and pricing, and determine which one is best for your business. Once you've chosen an autoresponder service, it's time to start thinking about email marketing strategies.

Chapter 2:
Email Marketing Strategies

There are a number of ways to leverage email marketing for your business. These range from super basic to super advanced and everything in between. Let's start by differentiating between the two main types of email marketing messages.

Newsletters

Newsletters are one of the oldest types of marketing models. Both in the case of print mail and email. Basically, you send out broadcasts to your list in "real-time" to notify them of offers, promotions, events, and any kind of updates. By "real-time" we mean specific dates on a calendar, rather than "X" number of days after subscribing. Newsletters are great because they provide a lot of flexibility, can be planned well in advance, and allow you to adjust your marketing and customer relationships "on the fly" based on what's going on in your industry at any given moment. Also, their "real-time" nature means everyone on your list is on the same page at any given time, which is great for moving large amounts of traffic at one time.

Autoresponder Sequences

Autoresponders are a predetermined series of emails that each new subscriber to your list gets after signing up. Where newsletters are great for producing massive effect at one time, autoresponders are great for easily ensuring every subscriber gets exposed to the same things in the same order. This means, regardless of real dates on a calendar, you can ensure that each lead gets the same message one the same numbered day in relation to when they subscribed. Bob, Ricky, and Sue will each get your "Top 3 Tools for Driving Traffic" promo email 4 days after they joined your list, regardless of when each of them joined.

If you have a handful of products that you want to ensure get offered to ALL of your subscribers after they opt-in to your list, then an autoresponder sequence is the way to accomplish that. Want to sequentially market 60 days' worth of affiliate products to each subscriber who joins your list and make sales on auto-pilot while you relax on the beach? Then a 60-day autoresponder sequence is the ticket. Welcome sequences, indoctrination sequences, webinar follow-ups, white-listing instructions… these are all things you'd use autoresponder messages for. And then, of course, the most basic function of an autoresponder message would be lead magnet delivery. Even if you don't use it for anything else in your marketing, you'll need it for at least that initial interaction in which you deliver the "free report" or whatever you use to get the subscriber on your list.

Combining Them

Ideally, a solid email marketing strategy will use a combination of newsletters and autoresponder sequences. At a minimum, you should have one robust welcome sequence in which you familiarize your subscriber with your brand, instruct them to white-list your email address and follow you on social, share your most popular helpful content, and anything else you think would help your business and your subscribers. Ideally, after that, you'd put them through at least a few cross-selling emails in which you introduce them to some of your own products or some affiliate offers (e.g. a "what we use" series might be a good way to help them by showcasing the tools you use in your business and earn some commissions at the same time if they decide to try those tools too). Once your autoresponder sequences are done, then it makes sense to drop your subscribers into a general pool of contacts who will simply receive your real-time newsletters from that point forward.

Frequency

A lot can be said about email marketing frequency. It's an area that divides marketers quite a bit. Generally, there are two opposing schools of thought plus a sort of "middle ground" position. Firstly, there is the "churn and burn" approach. This strategy basically means you mail your list very aggressively, at least daily, possibly multiple times daily, promoting affiliate products (usually current product launches), focusing on hard pitches and using things like scarcity tactics to get as many sales as possible. There's no question this will get you sales. But it can also kill your brand image.

The other approach is to mail less than daily, maybe even just 1 or 2 times per week, and to ensure you're not always selling something but, instead, making it a point to send out useful, free content regularly. This WOULD help set your brand apart and increase goodwill. But there's just one problem. Nobody will NOTICE your brand. We're living in a time where everyone is bombarded day and night with promo emails. If you're mailing so infrequently, there's a good chance you'll get lost in the ocean of competitor emails and not get noticed.

Then there's the middle ground. The middle ground approach acknowledges, on the one hand, that churn and burn is basically brand suicide. On the other hand, however, it also acknowledges that the "once or twice per week" approach will leave you largely unnoticed these days and doesn't generate much revenue. The middle ground, then, is to mail once-daily on average, with some exceptions being made sparingly for genuinely important scarcity-type events or promotions that might require two emails in one day. These mailings, however, should not all be sales promotions. A reasonable mix of hard sales, free useful content, and a hybrid "useful content with a subtle soft sales pitch" should be used. Ultimately, the appropriate frequency for mailing will depend a lot on your industry and your audience, but keep that general middle ground principle in mind when determining the right mailing plan for your business.

Upselling and Cross-selling

Probably one of the most obvious and financially rewarding aspects of email marketing is upselling or cross-selling. Typically, upselling means immediately offering a relevant product or service after the purchase of another product. The key words there are "immediate" and "relevant". In the digital world, this usually happens automatically as a buyer of a front-end product is then immediately forwarded to the next product in a sales funnel. But this can also be accomplished via email marketing by simply reminding buyers of the upsell and re-inviting them to buy it if they hadn't already. This means you'd want to set up your post-purchase autoresponder sequence (typically part of your welcome sequence) to include at least one email with a link to that upsell along with a restatement of the reasons the person should purchase it.

Cross-selling, on the other hand, can happen any time later in the customer relationship and does not need to involve products that are directly relevant, although some level of relevance would likely help. An example of cross-selling might be as follows. A customer or client purchases your CRM software. After two or three months of enjoying the software and maintaining a positive relationship with your business, you then invite them to look at your support desk software or your project management software. The offer happened later in the relationship and it was not directly relevant to CRM (well, the support desk one was a little bit related, but you get the idea).

Affiliate Marketing

It's important to note that, although upselling and cross-selling typically bring to mind your own products, that doesn't have to be the case. You can just as easily promote other businesses' offers and get paid affiliate commissions for the referrals. In fact, the majority of email marketers in the internet marketing niche do this almost exclusively. If you are a business with only one or two products of your own to offer, then affiliate marketing is likely the best way to make email marketing profitable for you. You can either approach other businesses or individuals directly for affiliate agreements, or you can use one of the many networks or marketplaces out there that are specifically designed to facilitate these relationships in a somewhat automated fashion. For digital products, for example, you might simply browse marketplaces like JVZoo, ClickBank, or WarriorPlus and request an affiliate link for any offers you think might be useful to your customers. For physical goods, you might have a look at a network like CommissionJunction or even major online giants like Amazon.com or Walmart.com. The key with affiliate marketing is to ensure the products are genuinely useful for your customers and to pitch them in a way that does not seem spammy.

Advanced Strategies

In recent years, email marketing has grown more complex and advanced. While you can still choose to focus only on the basic approaches revealed above, you may want to consider some of the more recent developments, like automation. Email marketing automation refers not simply to using an autoresponder sequence, but using a series of tools, triggers, and "if this then that" or IFTTT rules to create complex marketing processes and workflows that adapt themselves automatically to individual customers. This means you can create a workflow that not only sends a series of welcome/indoctrination messages to a new lead, but also automatically resends each message if the lead has not opened them after a certain period of time. You can then send leads through completely different automated sequences based on actions they took or failed to take. Did they click a link but not buy a product? Send them a message literally asking why they clicked but didn't buy and restating some product benefits or offering a discount. Did they attend a webinar but leave before the half-way point? Send a follow-up acknowledging that they left and offering a link to a replay. All of this would be done automatically by an automation system (which most, if not all, major autoresponder platforms offer these days).

Further advanced developments have been added to or incorporated into the recent automation trend. Scoring is a method by which your email platform applies a point value to certain actions (e.g. opening, clicking, buying) contributing to an overall score designed to give you a quick idea of how engaged or valuable a subscriber is. Tagging is another development and allows you a way of segmenting or distinguishing subscribers based on their behavior (e.g. the tag "attended webinar" could be applied to webinar attendees). This then allows you to take actions towards only specific groups who have been tagged with a certain tag. Both tagging and scoring can be incorporated into your automation workflows. For example, an automation could be created in which anyone tagged as "webinar attendee" would then be sent a promotional sequence offering products related to the topic covered in the webinar and anyone who hasn't opened your last 10 emails, and therefore drops below a certain scoring threshold could automatically be sent into a "re-engagement sequence" designed to get them opening your emails again. Finally, the ability of most automation platforms to utilize tracking pixels (as in the "did they buy" example above) as well as to integrate with other services (as in the webinar abandoner example above) makes the possibilities with email automation nearly endless.

Now that you have an idea of how to shape your email marketing strategy, you'll want to ensure every message you send is optimized to the max.

Chapter 3:
Marketing Optimization

Once you've established a strategy and are ready to begin email marketing, you'll want to ensure you optimize all of your email campaigns as much as possible to maximize your ROI. The first step is getting people to open your emails, and that starts with your subject line.

Subject Line Styles

Subject lines are absolutely critical. They are basically the bottleneck of all of your email marketing success. You need to convince people whose inboxes are full of promotional emails that yours is worth opening. And you've only got around 70 characters to do it (that's not a "hard limit", just happens to the case that almost nobody goes past around 70 characters). The other thing to consider is that a lot of people view their email of tablets and phones, so the visible characters are even fewer in those cases.

There are several different styles of subject lines to use. We'll discuss a handful of popular ones here. Firstly, there's the "benefit" subject line. This is where your subject line clearly states a benefit like "Drive more traffic and boost conversions". Then there's the opposite style: the "pain" subject line. This is where your subject line reminds subscribers of their problems, for example: "Does WordPress make you pull your hair out?" might be great if you're pitching a drag and drop web builder. The "story" subject line is another useful one and literally involves a line from a story, designed to get the reader to want to open your email, such as: "So I was walking my dog the other day when, suddenly…" Then there's the "blind" subject line, which means hinting at something compelling, but not revealing what it is and letting the mysteriousness draw people in. After that, there's the "shock" subject line, which mentions one noteworthy or shocking detail like "The president invited these affiliate marketers to the White House. Seriously." Finally, there's the "scarcity" approach which makes a person fearful of losing out, such as "Warning: Discount ends in 30 min – don't pay full price tomorrow".

Timing

The timing of your emails can be incredibly important. Contrary to popular belief, there are no secret "perfect times" to send emails that a group of gurus knows about but keeps to themselves. As cliché as the phrase "it depends" may sound, it truly and genuinely does depend on your list. Where are they? Is the email one you can expect them to open while at work? In other words, is it a business to consumer email or, if you're doing B2B sales, are they a business owner or head of a relevant office who can/will open your email any time during the work day? In this a business to consumer relationship, then your email would not be considered "work email" and therefore, you might want to mail either early in the morning, during lunch, or in the evening after the work day. Same goes for days of the week. Are you targeting retail shoppers? Then the end of the week might be the right time to announce a major weekend sale. At the end of the day, you'll need to pay close attention to what times seem to product the best results for your list and adjust accordingly. This will require some testing and analysis on your part.

Personalization

Personalization can be an incredibly effective tool in email marketing. It can be used in both subject lines and email bodies. In the case of subject lines, the use of a person's name has been shown to boost open rates by around 30%. Personalization can also, obviously be used in the body of your message and, particularly when used in the salutation, can help encourage your readers to keep on reading further. Personalization doesn't have to stop at a person's name, however. Any data you collected via an opt-in form, including location, age, gender, birthdays, relationship status, and so on can be utilized to personalize an email.

Body Styles

There are a thousand and one ways to write your message body. The styles we'll discuss here happen to mirror the subject line styles we discussed earlier. There's the story approach, in which you engage your readers and keep them reading to see how it ends. There's the shock style which introduces one shocking factor and entices the reader to click to find out more. The blind style is similar in that it claims something compelling but it doesn't need to be "shocking" per se, and also it tends not to reveal any significant factors, except for results, causing the reader to want to learn what tool or solution can lead to those results. The fear and scarcity style bodies tend to be short and sweet, emphasizing the "you're about to miss out" message. Finally, there are the full, long-form, presell style message bodies. This is where you're simply doing the necessary selling of a product idea before the reader even clicks the link to the offer. In this style, you typically touch on all the standard sales techniques, especially pain/problem, solution, benefit, call-to-action, and so on.

CTR Optimization

There are several tactics that can be used to optimize your click-through rate (CTR). The first has to do with link placement. Placing your link in a few different parts of your email body, such as between paragraphs, at the end, and again in the P.S., can be useful. However, depending on your audience, it might come off as overly aggressive and too many links may even trigger spam filters. Other useful elements that can help are hyperlinked images, gifs, and video-looking images with play buttons (make sure there's really a video on the other end). Also, actual visual CTA buttons rather than just textual links might boost your CTR, as might countdown timers.

As we've seen, there are countless factors that can affect your open rates and CTRs. The effect of each of these is completely dependent on your audience and it's critical to understand that many of the tactics that sound like a great idea and might work well with one audience, can actually HARM your performance in some cases. So, the key is to constantly be testing and analyzing. Specifically, make sure you test and analyze these things in isolation, not all at once, so you know what thing cause which effect. Once you've got some optimized email campaigns going, you'll need to ensure you're properly managing your email list and that's what we'll cover next.

Chapter 4:
Email List Maintenance

Practicing good email list maintenance is critical to keeping your deliverability up as well as keeping a happy healthy list overall. Low open rates, unsubscribes, complaints, inactive subscribers, and bad hygiene in general can severely impact your ability to get in the inbox and avoid the spam folder. It can also cause you to get on the bad side of your autoresponder service which can often mean having your account shut down and losing access to your list.

Lead Quality

The very first step in maintaining a healthy list is ensuring your leads are high quality to begin with. Studies have shown that up to 30% of contact info entered into opt-in forms is bogus. Furthermore, it's generally accepted that most people who do put a "real" email address in, don't put their best one in. Most people have a secondary email address that they don't check regularly and that they use exclusively for collecting lead magnets and promotional stuff. To maintain a healthy list and good email marketing stats, it's important that you try to make your leads as high quality as possible.

One way to do this is to use "confirmed" opt-in, also sometimes called "double opt-in". This way people have to click a "confirm your request for information" link in an initial email prior to being added to your list. This helps ensure you are getting real email addresses and that your subscribers will be less likely to forget that they indeed opted in to your list. However, although this solves the problem of FAKE emails, it does not quite solve the problem of SECONDARY or low quality email addresses. This also reduces the overall amount of leads added to your list (though most would argue the lead quality is worth the smaller number of leads).

One further approach to ensure your email addresses are high quality is to simply avoid traditional opt-in forms altogether. Various solutions exist for acquiring high quality contact data without relying on blank form fields. Facebook Lead Ads and Twitter Lead Cards are good ways to capture quality names and emails associated with people's social media accounts. Even better, tools like MobileOptin and Warlord Mobile Leads allow you to capture the name and email associated with a person's smartphone email account. Finally, building a buyers list with low-priced offers, in which contact info is derived from transaction data, is also an effective way to ensure your leads' contact info is legitimate and high quality.

Segmentation

An excellent way to maintain a healthy (and happy) list is to segment your subscribers. It's always likely that you have people in multiple niches, industries, and walks of life on your list. To help make sure your subscribers are only getting promotions that are relevant to them, it's a good idea to segment. For example, in the IM niche, you might have eCommerce store owners who sell physical goods as well as affiliate marketers who operate exclusively in the digital space. There's a good chance that multiple emails about things like affiliate marketing secrets, private label rights (PLR) products, and "make money online" opportunities would annoy the eCommerce store owners enough to mark as spam, complain, or unsubscribe. This hurts your list health and deliverability. If at all possible, you should try to segment your list at the very beginning by having certain form fields that identify industries at the time of opt-in, or by sending out surveys and so on later on.

List Hygiene

Trimming the fat and maintaining a lean, clean, engaged list can do wonders for your deliverability. The easiest and most hands-free way to do this is to ensure it is super easy for your subscribers to unsubscribe. If someone doesn't want to be on your list, then you shouldn't want them there either. Ensure that you have a clear and visible unsubscribe option in the header or footer of your emails. This ensures you don't have a bunch of resentful people on your list who ignore your emails (which hurts deliverability) and reduces the amount of people who feel the need to complain or hit the spam button (which hurts deliverability).

Another, more manual, way to clean your list is to get rid of disengaged followers yourself. If you have certain subscribers who have not opened any of your emails in the last few months, delete them! If you're using an advanced feature like scoring, then you can automatically have a subscriber who falls below a certain score be removed from your list. Your increase in open rates will dramatically improve the health of your list.

Battle Plan

Step 1: Test, compare, and choose an autoresponder that works for your business.

Step 2: Sit down and brain storm or research a list of products and services that you can either offer yourself or promote as an affiliate with email marketing.

Step 3: Draft up an email marketing plan consisting of autoresponder sequences, newsletter broadcasts, and any advanced features like automation and so on, if you feel comfortable with them.

Step 4: Once your email marketing apparatus is up and running, start implementing and testing various subject and body styles in order to optimize your campaign performance.

Step 5: Develop a monthly hygiene plan for keeping your list healthy and well-maintained.